KU-679-312

The Day
Before Yesterday

The Day Before Yesterday

A photographic album of daily life in
Victorian and Edwardian Britain

Introduced by Peter Quennell

Photographic research by Harold Chapman and Thelma Shumsky
Captions by Joanna Smith

J.M. Dent & Sons Ltd
London, Melbourne and Toronto

© John Topham Picture Library, 1978
All rights reserved
Printed and Bound in Great Britain by
William Clowes and Sons Ltd
London, Beccles and Colchester
for J.M. Dent & Sons Ltd
Aldine House, Albemarle Street, London
First published in the U.K. 1978

This book if bound as a paperback is subject to the
condition that it may not be issued on loan or otherwise
except in its original binding

British Library Cataloguing in Publication Data
The day before yesterday.
        1. Great Britain – Social life and customs –
        19th century – Pictorial works   2. Great Britain
        – Social life and customs – 20th century – Pictorial
        works
941.08′022′2   DA533

CONTENTS

with plate numbers

Introduction

In 1839 reports of a marvellous new discovery flashed
across the Western world. That year an English country
gentleman, William Henry Fox Talbot, and a French
scene-painter, Louis Jacques Mandé Daguerre, announced
the results of many years' work, and the first photographs
(then called calotypes and daguerreotypes) excited general
admiration. Although the two inventors had been working along completely separate lines, they had set out to
solve the same problem – how to fix the image cast by the
old-fashioned *camera obscura*,★ the fascinating device that
Leonardo da Vinci had discussed in his note-books and a
late-sixteenth-century Neapolitan savant, Giovanni Bat-
tista della Porta, had apparently perfected. The *camera
obscura* provided a lively reflection of nature; and numerous artists, including Canaletto, had found it an invaluable
aide; but its images were transitory. Talbot and Daguerre
believed that, with the help of chemicals sensitive to light,
they could be caught and fixed for ever; and, after lengthy
trials, each succeeded, Daguerre making use of metal and,
subsequently, glass plates, Talbot of chemically-coated
sheets of paper. Whereas daguerreotypes were impossible
to reproduce, Talbot's method had one conspicuous
advantage; his paper sheets were the equivalent of a modern photographic negative; and his calotypes were reproduced at will.

Such was the birth of an art that has immeasurably
enriched our lives. Both pioneers chose to publish books –
Daguerre, a treatise entitled *Historique et description des
procédés du daguerréotype;* Talbot, *The Pencil of Nature*, the
earliest book to contain photographic illustrations.
Daguerre, almost as soon as he announced his discoveries,
reaped tremendous popular renown; and in 1840 a satirical

★   The *camera obscura* is described in a modern reference-book as 'a light-tight
   box or chamber with a convex lens at one end and a screen, on which an
   image is produced, at the other'.

print appeared that showed a vast crowd of prospective clients fighting its way into his studio, and a train and a steamboat standing by, prepared to carry his invention to the furthest corners of the earth. Some of Talbot's pictures possess a rare beauty – he found a multitude of delightful subjects near his ancient Wiltshire country house. But neither he nor Daguerre was a true imaginative artist; and they were quickly followed by a series of very much more gifted men; for example, by David Octavius Hill, the Scottish painter turned photographer, who, between 1843 and 1848, created a succession of extraordinarily moving and dramatic portraits; and by Nadar, otherwise Félix Tournachon, an indefatigable French enthusiast, who, during the next decade, immortalized every distinguished personality he could persuade to face his lens – among his sitters were Baudelaire, Balzac, George Sand, the brothers Goncourt, Delacroix, Rossini, Berlioz and the Russian revolutionary Bakunin – and thus built up a splendid pictorial survey of mid-nineteenth-century life and literature.

It was Nadar's purpose, he said, to 'raise photography to the level of an art'. But one of the attractions of the new art was that, besides its aesthetic value, it had a strong historical appeal. Here was an opportunity of arresting the passage of time, of conferring a distinct and durable form upon our fugitive impressions of the present day, and enabling every man to act as his own chronicler. This opportunity the Victorian Age seized. Not only did clever professionals abound; but countless amateurs recorded their families and friends and the buildings and landscapes that they loved best. Some of them were celebrated in other fields, like the Reverend Charles Lutwidge Dodgson, better known as Lewis Carroll, a keen photographer of the little girls who cheered his celibate existence. Their products, stuck into innumerable albums, show varying degrees of skill; but, now and then, the hobby that had amused their leisure moments became an obsessive life-long passion.

Particularly interesting is the case of Francis Frith. Born in 1822 at Chesterfield, today a populous industrial centre, but during his boyhood, he tells us, 'a pretty country town, as stagnant as one of those secluded fish-ponds of the last century . . . full of rank greenery, and lazy, insipid carp and tench', he belonged to a middle-class Quaker family, and had inherited their solid virtues. Frith's father had been a cooper by trade, a manufacturer of casks and barrels. Frith himself, however, moved away to Liverpool, where he launched a wholesale grocery firm, but presently sold the business and, when he was about thirty-four, retired 'with a moderate fortune'.* His second venture, a local printing company, soon proved even more successful. By 1856 Frith was rich enough to spend several months exploring Egypt; and he financed further expeditions in 1857 and 1859. On all his journeys he carried three cameras and a cumbersome load of photographic apparatus. His main object, when he visited Egypt, Palestine, Greece and Turkey, was to photograph their scenes and peoples.

Frith had a visionary character; that is evident from his descriptions of his early life, in which he often reminds us of Samuel Palmer and Edward Calvert, Blake's most promising young disciples. He, too, received his spiritual education from his study of the English landscape. 'The memories of my boyhood', he wrote, 'are very largely of fields and streams and green lanes'; and his recollections of the school-room were shadowy, 'compared with that of a certain gigantic pear-tree in my father's garden, amid whose branches I spent many a rare umbrageous hour, and innumerable bits of picturesque hill and dale where I wandered and fished and "muttered my wayward fancies" through long summer days of half unconscious happiness, drinking in at every pore of nerve and soul the poetry of nature, and nursing into wild and vigorous growth . . . every inborn faculty of person and mind that I can recognize as specialities of my constitution.'

Elsewhere he gives us an extremely vivid account of the nervous collapse that seemed about to overwhelm him as he neared the age of twenty-one. His state of mind was alarming indeed. It resembled 'the moment in a hunter's life when, after infinite pains, and weary watching to find

* In an excellent biography of Frith, *Victorian Cameraman* (1973), to which I have been much indebted, the author, Mr Bill Jay, suggests that he may have earned his 'moderate fortune', not in the wholesale grocery business, as he asserted in his reminiscences, but in his second undertaking.

his game, it faces him at last in the moonlight, huge and indistinct'. The tension of his mind and soul were so acute that 'my health, which had never been robust, broke down under the strain, and my nervous system . . . shook me with a pitiless energy which threatened both life and reason'.

Apart from these early crises, his successes as a businessman and his journey through the Middle East, Frith's career was not eventful. He contracted a happy marriage, sired a large family and – always an extremely handsome man, with bright eyes, a high, unwrinkled forehead and a fine Victorian beard – acquired a nobly patriarchal look. Established at a pleasant house in Reigate, he now assumed the direction of a thriving photographic firm. His Egyptian pictures and the two books in which he bound them up, *Cairo, Sinai, Jerusalem and the Pyramids of Egypt* and *Egypt and Palestine*, were widely sold and much praised. His photographs, declared *The Times*, 'carry us far beyond anything that is in the power of the most accomplished artist to transfer to his canvas'; and, when he attended a meeting of the Photographic Society, he received a rapturous welcome.

His last major project was to execute a detailed survey of Great Britain as a whole, and market his photographs throughout the country in the form of inexpensive picture postcards. It was a bold scheme; and he hired a team of assistants who followed him upon his travels – he was also accompanied by his wife and children and three or four domestic servants – and helped him to extend his territorial scope. Of the photographs reproduced here a large proportion are the work of Francis Frith, or were no doubt inspired by him; and together they afford us a panoramic view of the late-Victorian British landscape, which was then slowly changing, as the century approached its end, and losing its antique charm under the stern pressure of modern industrial developments. The collection ranges from pictures taken in the 1860s to entertaining glimpses of Edwardian social life; and, since I was born early in 1905, I often feel, while I examine these plates, that I am revisiting my own past, and half expect to see myself portrayed there, on a Norfolk beach, walking along a lane, visiting a parish church, or seated at my elders' feet in a

'Wedding Group' of 1910. I recognize the straw boaters, the ladies' voluminous skirts, the homely carts and traps and stately carriages.

Frith was especially fond of country towns; and my parents lived near a market-town some ten or fifteen miles from London. London's suburbs were quickly to swallow it up, and destroy its previous character. In my early childhood it was a mixture of old and new; but my mother distinctly remembered a period when it still retained a rustic air; and an elderly friend, who was settled not far away, kept a pack of fox hounds and used to bowl through Bromley High Street driving a smart high-wheeled gig. The sheaf of reminiscences she wrote in her old age frequently recall a photograph by Frith or one of his Edwardian successors; and, as they were never published, though she prepared a slender pamphlet for private circulation only, some passages seem worth transcribing.

Above all else, they suggest that the life of an English market-town in the 1890s was far more variegated than it is today; the tradesman and the artisan continued to be distinguished by the professional uniform he wore and the tools he carried round with him. Nowadays it is difficult to tell the electrician from the builder's labourer; but there was no mistaking the Victorian navvy for the carpenter or butcher's boy. The sooty-faced sweep cut a strangely picturesque figure; and my mother's first memory was of being taken out into the garden, after a heavy fall of snow, to see his bristling black brush suddenly emerge above the chimney-pots – a treat, she says, that made her scream.

Then there was the lamp-lighter, who 'came to the path in front of our house . . . and pushed a long rod up the column to the lamp', and whose regular arrival, unlike that of the sweep, was always comforting and reassuring. Showmen and pedlars repeatedly passed the gate – the organ-grinder, who trundled his organ along, with a red-jacketed monkey perched on the box, or, at his heels, a troupe of little performing dogs; the hurdy-gurdy man, who ground out popular songs; or the itinerant proprietor of a Punch-and-Judy show. Gypsies and girls selling sprigs of dried lavender often visited the house. In the windows of the gypsies' caravans 'usually hung a lace curtain . . . and round the van were slung brushes and brooms . . . baskets, trugs and clothes' pegs . . . The men wore corduroys, the women a wide skirt and shawl; and their hair, parted in the middle, was plaited into narrow braids, the end of each braid fastened to the beginning to form a loop. These loops hung all around their faces. In bad weather they hooded themselves with a coloured handkerchief . . .'

Autumn and winter evenings were enlivened by the appearance of the muffin-man, ringing his bell, a tray of muffins and crumpets, under a green baize cloth, expertly balanced on his head. But the occasions to which my mother most looked forward were festivals that engrossed the whole town. Thursday was market-day, when neighbouring farmers set up their stalls about the spacious market-square, selling butter and cheese, fruit and vegetables, farmhouse-bread, new-laid eggs and a special delicacy called 'lardy cake'. Toys and sweets were sold there, too – balloons, paper windmills, sugar-mice; while elsewhere industrious silk-worms could be bought at five a penny.

Even in semi-suburban Bromley the old traditions died hard; and on May 1st a procession of village children, 'pushing a small goat-cart with flowers arranged all over it, and carrying a long stick with a bouquet tied at the top and a rope of flowers round the pole', made a circuit of the streets and sang their ancient pagan ditty:

> The first of May is Flora's day
> Because it is a flowery day.
> Please to remember the maypole,
> Please to remember the garland.

'At home' (my mother writes) 'we loved public holidays, my brothers and I; for Nurse always took us to see the Costermongers' Parade . . . Three or four large horse-brakes came up the hill to the Tiger's Head . . . and the Costermongers tumbled out . . . The men in suits covered with pearl buttons . . . The women in bright wide-shirted dresses and hats with long, brilliantly coloured ostrich feathers. The horses were decorated with ribbons and with all kinds of brass ornaments. The Costers crowded into the inn for drinks; after which they formed a large ring outside and danced to the music of accordions played by two men in the centre. Finally, the music stopped, the crowd broke up, and everyone clambered again into the brakes and set off towards Keston Common where they held their yearly fair.'

The present volume includes a couple of photographs of nineteenth-century fire-engines; and my mother remembered a tremendous drama when, 'on our way to the shops, we heard behind us a loud bell ringing and men shouting, and the clattering of hooves; and up the hill came a pair of magnificent dapple grey horses, galloping at full speed . . . The fire-engine was manned by shouting firemen . . . All the traffic pulled to the sides of the road, and my brothers shouted too . . .'

My mother's childhood seldom lacked excitement; and, a circus having pitched its tents near the town, an unforeseeable adventure was provided by a baby elephant that broke loose and wandered away from the circus, and terrified a little neighbour by thrusting its diminutive trunk (which he mistook for a monstrous grey arm) across his parents' garden-hedge. Compared with her youth, my mother regarded the background of her later years as sadly flat and colourless; and these photographs indicate that her affection for the past was not entirely misguided. The England they reveal was far more idiosyncratic, more various and rich in detail, than the country that we know today. But it was also less humane. The division between the classes, between the workman and the gentleman, the very rich and the very poor, was still formidably clear-cut; and a photograph taken during the great London dock-strike of 1889 reminds us that the period in which she grew up was one of fierce industrial conflict. She was only five when the dockers went on strike; but her father, whose business was shipping – he was a fairly successful ship-broker – must have watched it with alarm.

The struggle concerned a single penny. Hitherto, some 90,000 of London's dock-workers were employed upon a part-time basis; for many ships they served were still under sail; and their arrival or non-arrival was dictated by the winds. Thus, every morning at six o'clock, a huge concourse of work-hungry men assembled round the dock-gates, clamouring to be allowed to earn a daily wage of five pence an hour, and seven pence an hour overtime.

Their leader Ben Tillett now demanded a rate of sixpence and eightpence, and that they should be guaranteed four hours' employment. But the dock-companies, whose economic position was temporarily difficult, decided that they must refuse; and by 13 August 1889, the men had announced that they would stop work.

At one point a General Strike was planned, though the plan was never carried through. Meanwhile, under the leadership of John Burns (later, Privy Councillor and Cabinet Minister) who had come to Tillett's aid, a regiment of 12,000 pickets was enlisted, and daily marches were organized through the City to the West End. The Australian Labour movement contributed £24,000 to the dockers' strike-fund; and General Booth and the Salvation Army gave their powerful assistance. The marches were orderly; but the Docks became a battle-ground; and the battles fought behind their walls left a legacy of savage ill-feeling. At last, the employers gave way, and their employees won 'the Dockers' Tanner'. The promised sixpence brought them back to work; and in the yards and the slums surrounding them an uneasy peace reigned.

On other fields, at the close of the nineteenth century, more pacific conflicts took place. George Bernard Shaw, whose *Fabian Essays* appeared in 1889, was taking up arms against Victorian conservatism; and Walter Pater and Oscar Wilde sought to undermine the philistine prejudices of the British middle classes. H.G. Wells' exciting scientific romances, of which the earliest, *The Time Machine*, came out in 1895, were succeeded by his tendentious social novels; and *Love and Mr Lewisham*, published in 1900, aimed a shrewd blow at the orthodox conception of marriage.

I am too young to have suffered much myself from the Victorian and Edwardian moral code. But I was aware of its existence. I knew that my nanny had somehow 'got into trouble', and been obliged to leave our household, and that a French governess had gone the same way. In 1911, when my parents attended a performance of Diaghilev's new *Ballets Russes*, they found *Shéhérazade* slightly shocking; and there was a large number of subjects and persons that they thought it best to leave unmentioned. Tabus encompassed us; ours was a very small and perhaps a somewhat sanctimonious world; and we were sharply hostile towards aristocratic Society and its self-indulgent goings-on, of which we heard through newspapers and magazines. Proud to belong to the innocent middle class, we unquestioningly embraced its standards.

Physically, life was good. We ate abundant meals; and obliging local tradesmen carried our provisions to the door. The butcher's boy regularly took our orders, and returned with the meat in his employer's cart. The baker's attendance was no less regular; and the milkman, who wore a striped apron, drove every day around the neighbourhood, transporting a huge lidded vessel, from which the quantity of milk we needed was measured out into our own jugs. We had three servants, besides our nanny and, at times, a governess. The cook and the parlour-maid each received £35 a year, according to my mother's narrative, and the housemaid £25; and all wore, as custom demanded, black stuff dresses and neatly starched caps. 'A boy', my mother adds, 'came three times a week for two shillings a time, cleaned the knives in a large circular machine, and cleaned and polished boots and shoes.'

The mistress of the household was expected to superintend the morals and manners of her servants; and my mother relates how, as an inexperienced young married woman, she was once taken to task by an officious elderly acquaintance, who 'asked me if I knew that my cook had gone out on her "afternoon-off" in a red coat and skirt. Could I not stop her appearing so terribly "fast". The coat and skirt was of a very pretty rose-red'; and my mother, with more determination than she often displayed, bravely refused to reprimand the cook. 'I told her that I thought that she looked nice and very pretty . . .'

Neither of my parents was a disciplinarian; I and my sister were remarkably well treated. But it now strikes me – a point confirmed by some of these photographs – that we were almost always over-dressed. My sister, for instance, during her nursery and school-room days, frequently wore a ridiculous lace bonnet; and the little Edwardian girls depicted in the present collection exhibit buttoned boots and thick stockings, many-layered skirts and petticoats and big flimsy wide-brimmed hats, a replica of contemporary adult modes. There was a certain stuffiness, I cannot help feeling, about the atmosphere in which we lived. So much comfort, so much security, such a wealth of minor blessings tended to befog the social climate; and any threats of unrest that reached our ears sounded distant and unreal.

True, militant suffragettes were demanding 'Votes for Women', invading parliament, assaulting cabinet ministers and pouring corrosive fluid into pillar-boxes; and I was amused and delighted myself to receive a letter of which the envelope had been partly burned away. Then, on the eve of the Great War, another controversy flared up; and the opponents of Irish Home Rule, headed by Edward Carson, brought the country, historians tell us, to the verge of civil strife. Although my school-fellows presented me with a large button, bearing the aggressive legend '*Support Loyal Ulster*', which I boldly wore in my lapel, my parents, so far as I can remember, were not very much perturbed.

Nor did we immediately grasp the significance of events in August 1914; the war, we believed, would soon be over; and our placid daily life went on, while I arranged rows of little coloured flags across a map of Northern France. Alas, the line of Allied flags was perpetually falling back. In 1915 my father sold the house that he had built in 1906, and that my mother dearly loved; and we retired to a rented house below a railway-embankment, where ammunition trucks, bound for the battle-fields, rumbled ominously through the night. Expelled from our snug suburban paradise, we joined the growing army of the new poor.

Peter Quennell

Growing up

1. Mothers with their babies at the Infants' Hospital, Westminster; c.1908. By this time infant mortality, the scourge of earlier generations, had decreased sharply, largely because of better sanitation and water supply, but also because of better nursing.

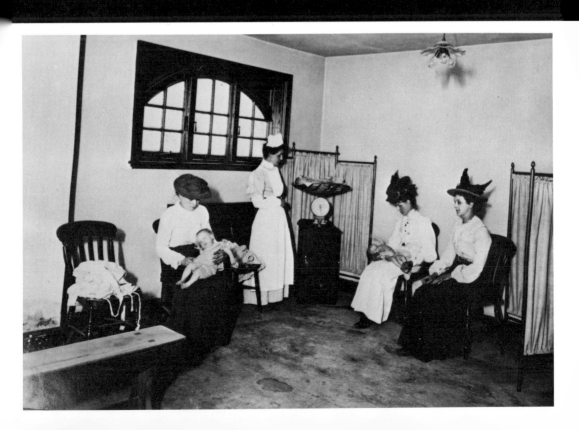

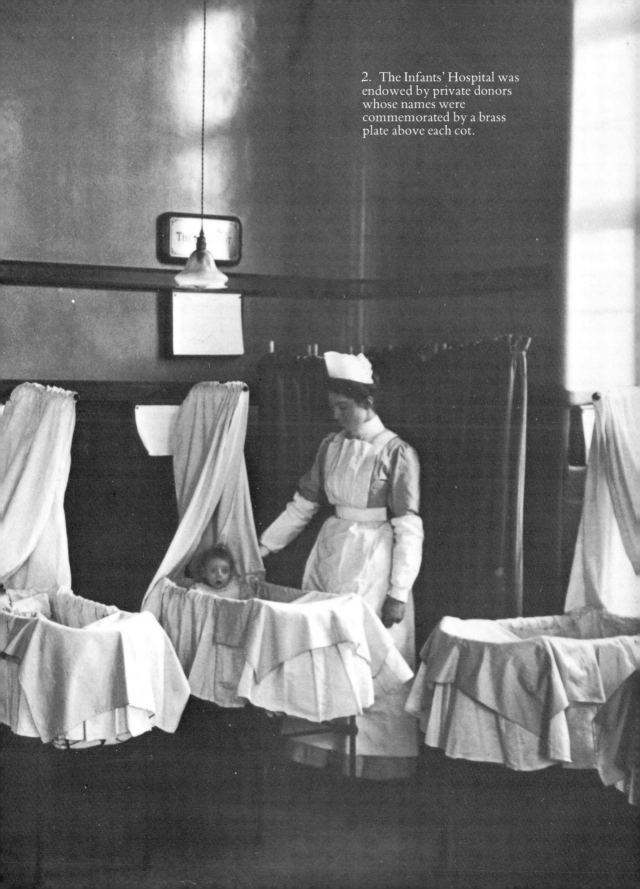

2. The Infants' Hospital was endowed by private donors whose names were commemorated by a brass plate above each cot.

▲ 3. A very unusual
photograph of a cottage
interior, c.1900: the one
candlestick, the bare floor
and lack of furniture, the
baby in a basket on the floor,
and the shabby clothing tell
much about growing up for a
labourer's son in the country
at the turn of the century; a
far cry from the roses and
honeysuckle and
neatly-dressed villagers
beloved of artists and art
photographers of the period.
Yet the man could afford his
newspaper and the china
dogs on the mantel would be
prized items today.
Agricultural wages at this
time were between fifteen
and twenty shillings a week.

▶ 4. Bath-time for toddlers,
c.1900.

◀ 5. A respectable family group, c.1906. Children were always far too warmly dressed. 'It fairly makes my heart bleed to see photograph after photograph of ourselves, as children, playing in the garden in high summer, always in thick black woolly stockings and high boots' (Gwen Raverat in *Period Piece*). Dressing was a long affair for all ages, for every garment (and all wore several layers) was fastened by rows of tiny buttons.

▼ 6. A Noah's ark on the chair, beautifully-made animals on the table, a superior-looking doll in the armchair. One of Sutcliffe's photographs, taken about 1890 to experiment with the new Kodak cameras.

7. Two girls washing their
dolls' clothes, imitating their
nurses, who spent hours of
their time washing, sewing
and ironing.

8. Dolls were even more elaborately dressed than their owners. This baby carriage in 1889 was obviously home-made as were so many children's toys.

9. The hay wain, c.1910, going out to the hayfield empty except for a load of delighted children, probably farm workers' children.

▲10. No plastic buckets in this sandpit, but miniature metal buckets and spades.

▶ 11. The Grammar School, Shepton Mallet, 1899. Then, as now, a photographer in search of sales for his prints would photograph a school and the forms confident that every pupil would buy at least one photograph. The building could be divided by sliding glass screens – the tracks can be seen overhead – into individual classrooms or, as appropriate, the screens could be pushed back, the furniture rolled to one side and the entire space used. Many desks of this sort would have sliding tops to accommodate pupils of different sizes.

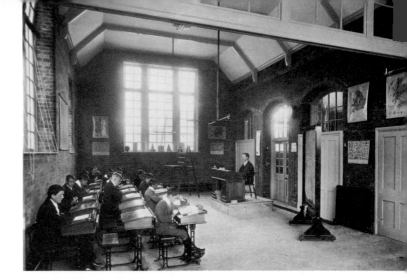

▶ 12. St John's School, Battersea in 1903. The Act of 1870 provided that there must be a school within the reach of every child in the country; in 1880 education became compulsory and from 1891 it was provided free of charge. St John's was typical of the new type of school which was being built – many of which still survive. Most children in the 1890s would leave before they were thirteen.

▶ 13. Schoolboys at Looe, Cornwall in 1906, dressed up for the occasion. These would have been for the most part sons of fishermen or indeed of smugglers; they look a tough lot!

14. Plymouth, Mutley, Western College, c.1890. Founded in 1752 for the training of Congregational Ministers, it moved to Plymouth in 1844. The buildings in the photograph were erected in 1861, and still exist today. The college itself moved to Bristol in 1907, where it has remained ever since.

15. A row of boater-hatted girls had made clothes for their dolls, displayed for the photographer, while the rest of the class went on with their knitting. The school mistress looks on sternly.

16. A cooking class in 1910 – learning how to make apple turnovers.

17. Dancing around the maypole c.1900. Probably this was a school treat; it certainly was not a genuine survival of the old custom.

18. The schoolroom of the St Marylebone Charity School for Girls in 1890. Here children of respectable working-class parents were given an education which was to fit them for becoming domestic servants; but they were also taught music by the tonic sol-fa method. These girls were doing sums on squeaky slates.

19. More stockings and boots, and of course the regulation hat, for this little girl on her tricycle.

20. A carefully posed photograph of North Parade, Barnstaple; even the policeman in the background co-operated. The delightful, curly, wicker perambulator and push chair would already have been considered rather old-fashioned when the photograph was taken in 1906.

▶ 21. Aylesbury Canal in the 1890s. Canal traffic had much declined, but for these children there were still some working boats to watch, fish to be caught, rubbish to be investigated.

22. Leaning over the bridge:
another informal snapshot
which Sutcliffe took for
Kodak.

▲ 23. The stepping stones across the River Rothay near Ambleside, in the Lake District, are still there and still much photographed. The young lady's skirts were, for the time, short.

▶ 24. Pangbourne, Berkshire in 1900. A girl takes her bonneted sister to H. Sellwood's Riverside Stores. It was an article of faith that if the sun's rays touched the back of the neck, sunstroke would surely follow.

▼ 25. Prizes at the fair, c.1898 – taken for Kodak by Paul Martin, perhaps the most successful of the informal Victorian photographers. The children's faces suggest this assembly of toys and books was the Victorian equivalent of a modern tombola.

◄ 26. Expectant faces at a Mothering Sunday parade, c.1898. The custom had its origin in previous centuries when maids in service were given a Sunday off in mid-Lent to visit their mothers and took with them a special cake.

◄ 27. Young girls sitting with their needlework. Almost all girls and women had their 'work' which went with them practically everywhere. Doctors in the 1890s were writing articles pressing girls to leave their work behind when they were in the fresh air, and to take more exercise.

▼ 28. After school – Windsor Castle in the background, 1889.

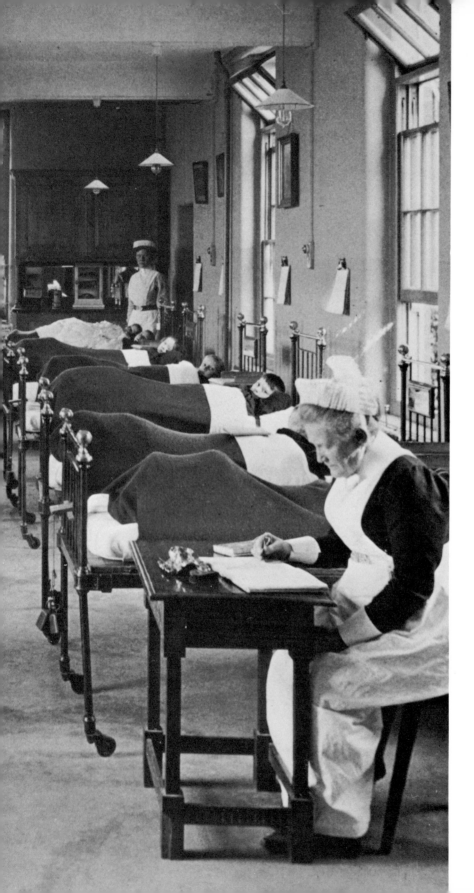

Alexandra Hospital, East Clandon, for the treatment of children with hip diseases c.1910. The interior shot (29) shows the matron writing her notes. The beds could be wheeled out during the day onto the verandah (30), a refreshing change from the days when fresh air was thought to be positively dangerous.

31. Poor children were expected to work from an early age. These two boys were selling onions in Plymouth, c.1907.

◀ 32. Queen Victoria's Jubilee Celebrations of 1887 had obviously exhausted the goats that drew this little goat cart. Goat carts were often seen at the seaside as an amusement for children.

▼ 33. Donkeyrides were also popular with children but on this occasion at Burnham, c.1910, the sailor's girlfriend also wanted to have a go.

▶ 34. A delightful holiday snap at Newquay, in Cornwall, c.1914. Sea water was supposed to have almost magic properties and many nurses would put a handful of sea salt in the children's baths when they were not at the seaside.

▶ 35. Playing on the beach, c.1910. How did their hats stay on? Notice the sailor suit which was immensely popular at the time.

36. One of Sutcliffe's photographs of naked boys playing at the water's edge. Boys commonly bathed naked, and this was accepted – but to photograph the practice was another matter and Sutcliffe got into trouble for it when his famous photograph 'The Water Rats', was exhibited in 1887. Sutcliffe was excommunicated by the local clergy – but the Prince of Wales ordered a big enlargement and hung it in Marlborough House.

37. A holiday at Weymouth
in 1909. The clock was
erected in honour of Queen
Victoria's Jubilee. Some of
the children are wearing
life-savers under their
clothes.

Hard Work

38 and 39. Building the London Underground at Baker Street in the 1860s. The chief engineers involved in the first Underground railways were Sir John Fowler and Sir Benjamin Baker, first Fowler's assistant and later his partner. Baker summed up: 'It is now known . . . how to underpin walls and, if necessary, carry the railway under houses and within a few inches of the kitchen floor without pulling down anything . . .' But it was agreed that the method was too expensive and later underground railways were of the deep-level tube-line type.

▲ 40. Quarrying granite near
Liskeard in Cornwall, with a
steam engine to transport the
blocks away, cranes and
pulleys for handling. The
workmen have decent sheds
for shelter.

▶ 41. King Edward Mine,
Camborne, Cornwall,
c.1906. Until the 1870s
Cornwall was the richest
source of copper and tin in
the world. The winding gear
and pumping engines
developed for the Cornish
mines were sophisticated and
powerful; examples of
engineering can be seen
today at Pool, preserved by
the National Trust, and at
the Holman Museum in
Camborne.

42. Oakley slate quarries, Blaenau Ffestiniog, Wales. The top of 'C' incline.

43. Slate splitters, c.1901 at Oakely Quarries, Blaenau Ffestiniog, Gwynedd. This highly skilled job is still carried on by a handful of craftsmen; it is a seasonal job, as frosts are used to widen the cracks and enable the slates to split more easily.

44. Repairing a church at Peterborough, c.1905.

45. Coming up for dinner from the pit. In the 1880s four miners, on average, were killed every day.

46. A cider flagon complements this man-sized meal for Cornish miners, c.1906, but the pasties were stuffed mainly with vegetables.

47. Salt workers at Droitwich in Worcestershire, which has natural brine springs known since Roman times; it still functions as a spa.

48. Herbal factory for making cough lozenges, c.1900: another reminder of the foul, polluted air which until recently kept the British population coughing so much so that bronchitis was called 'the English disease'.

▼ 49. Fitters' shop at the
Kodak factory, Harrow,
c.1907; in spite of the great
innovations in mechanical
engineering throughout the
nineteenth century,
handcraftmanship remained
highly important,
particularly in the fitting
shop.

50. Print finishing inspection, Kodak Harrow factory, c.1897: Kodak was at this time under its enterprising Managing Director, George Davison, one of the foremost photographers of his day. It was he who commissioned such fine photographers as Paul Martin and Frank Sutcliffe so that Kodak could use the results for their publicity. Davison incidentally was an active anarchist. He rented the top floor of Kodak's headquarters to a revolutionary association and financed their journal, *The Anarchist*. As a result he was persuaded to resign in 1912 by George Eastman, the American founder of the company.

51. A laundry worker in the wash-house of the Horton Asylum, c.1904.

52. Steam crane for unloading wood c.1895. Steam power was used not only for locomotives and traction engines, but also for fire engines, trams, excavators, steam hammers and even for domestic sewing machines.

53. A building site in the 1860s.

54. The big water wheel at Ironbridge, 1892.

◀ Loading barrels onto the distillery cart of the Thames Bank brewery in London (55); the brewery workers pose outside the factory (56).

◀ 57. Fish porters at Billingsgate, 1890, wearing headgear very different from the cork 'titfers' of the present day.

▶ 58. Building Rotherhithe Tunnel, 1905.

▼ 59. Old gas mains being replaced with new elliptical ones, prior to the electrification of the tramways, at the corner of Commercial Street and Whitechapel High Street, London, 1906.

60. A fisherman at Newlyn in Cornwall, c.1906, carrying a plummet line for mackerel and wearing leather sea boots. The buttons on his oilskins were very unusual; fishermen did not care for buttons, which could get caught in lines or nets.

61. Grimsby docks, c.1903. The boat is a steam trawler, with a steadying sail. The planks on board were to divide the catch to keep it from slipping around in the hold; they would have been brought up for cleaning. The fish were brought ashore in baskets, covered with ice.

62. Weighing fish at the fish scales, at Polperro, Cornwall, c.1888.

63. Skinning dogfish at Plymouth c.1906. Today's regulations would not allow the men to throw the fish on the ground.

64. Landing the catch at St
Ives, Cornwall, c.1900. The
tide was too low for the
luggers to come in.

65. Scottish herring girls at Whitby – a really messy job. Fish scales covered the ground. The man in the bowler hat was probably the salesman.

66. Herring fishermen at Deal with their catch. The nets were drift nets which floated like curtains with buoys on the top and weights at the bottom.

67. Three of the men in this picture are wearing Scotch bonnets, and the roller against the hatch coaming shows that the boat was working drift nets for herring. Probably a visiting Scots boat following the herring shoals south.

68. Loading the catch at St Ives, Cornwall, c.1900. The catch was probably pilchards, for which St Ives was famous.

Plying a Trade

69. A telephone exchange, c.1900. The telegraph and telephone service did a great deal for girls who had to go out to work. In the 1880s and 1890s domestic service had provided almost the only openings; by the time of this photograph women were in great demand as telephonists and also typists.

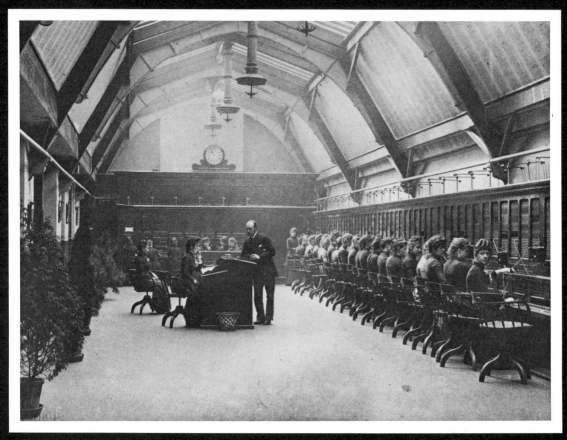

70. Ingleton, Yorkshire, 1888 – then dependent on small-scale industry, now a tourist centre for the West Riding. Like so many others the printers and stationers sold Frith's photographs, for since the 1860s Francis Frith & Co. had been the biggest photographic publishers in the world. While visiting the stationers, shoppers could buy sweetmeats from the vending machine or learn their correct weight.

71. The Three Choughs Hotel at Yeovil, c.1905, had its own turnout, but proudly announced 'Motor Accommodation'. In the archway stand members of the hotel staff.

► 73. Smith and Palmer hired out deckchairs on the beach at Southwold, Suffolk. Here is Mr Palmer himself, in front of his premises in 1902.

▼ 72. The comfortable office at no. 11, Charing Cross Road, complete with roll-top desk and Turkish carpet. The division of space may seem rather unequal to us, but was quite natural at the turn of the century.

74. In an age when almost all
heating came from open
fires, the sweeps were kept
busy cleaning the chimneys
which poured out coal
smoke over towns and cities,
bringing fog and grime and
bronchitis. As a Bradford
paper put it:

'How beautiful is the
    smoke
The Bradford smoke:
Pouring from
    numberless chimney
    stacks,
Condensing and falling
    in showers of blacks . . .'

75. Mush fakers and ginger
beer sellers on Clapham
Common in 1877. John
Thomson, 1837-1921, who
took this photograph, is
famous for his powerful
images of poverty: this
picture shows a ginger beer
stall in 1877. The big ginger
beer jar, which can be seen in
the basket, would fetch a
fancy price in a junk shop
today. It was estimated that
300,000 gallons of ginger
beer were sold in London
every summer. Mush fakers
were umbrella menders.

76. It looks as though it is raining, but the ice-cream vendor has in fact covered his ornate and beautiful cart with a striped, fringed awning. Ice cream may have been beautifully presented but it was made in very unhygienic conditions. Saffron Hill in London had a large colony of Italian ice-cream sellers, mostly from Calabria; they were often very prosperous.

77. The lamplighter vanished with the coming of electricity. This one in Colchester, c.1890, is trimming the lamp. For most of the nineteenth century gas lamps were dim and primitive in design and it was not until the 1880s that an effective gas lamp with the incandescent mantle was invented in response to the growing competition from electricity.

78. A cripple selling cough preventatives for 6d per packet and peppermints at the same price, 1877. Many of these street sellers of cough cures could only make a living at it in the winter.

▲ 79. The knife grinder has set himself up outside this pub in Eversley, Hampshire, with some of the staff lined up to watch the photographer. The knife grinder's machine was pedal-operated; he would push it from village to village where the inhabitants would bring him shears and scissors as well as knives to be sharpened.

◀ 80. H. Smith, tinman and cutler, on Wimbledon Common c.1898. His chief work was sharpening knives.

▶ 81. The sherbet seller c.1895. Paul Martin, unrecognized in his own day, has now won acclaim for his informal snapshots of daily life. He disguised his camera originally by covering it with brown paper and then in an unobtrusive leather case.

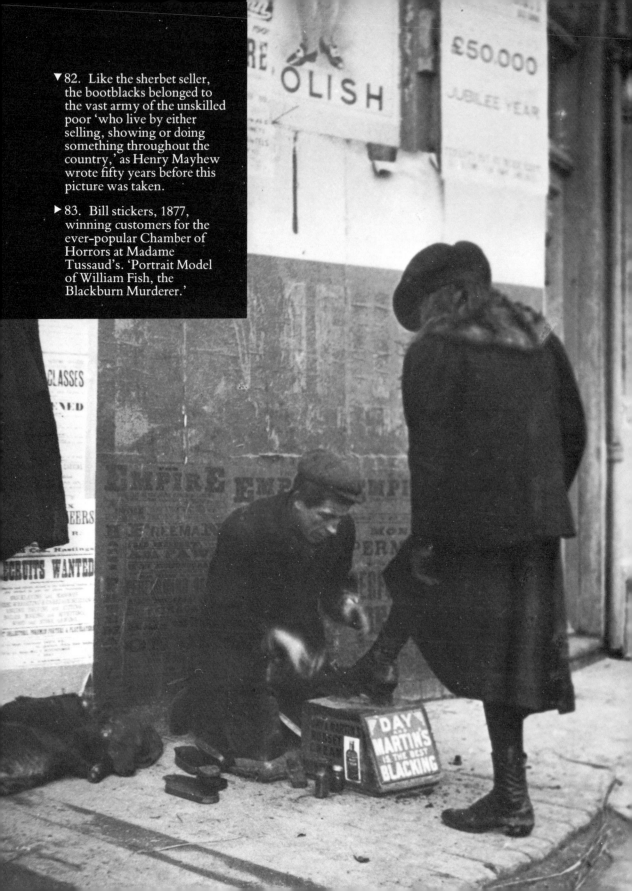

82. Like the sherbet seller, the bootblacks belonged to the vast army of the unskilled poor 'who live by either selling, showing or doing something throughout the country,' as Henry Mayhew wrote fifty years before this picture was taken.

83. Bill stickers, 1877, winning customers for the ever-popular Chamber of Horrors at Madame Tussaud's. 'Portrait Model of William Fish, the Blackburn Murderer.'

◄ 84. Steeplejacks
   photographed c.1900,
   probably near Reading.

► 85. The cobbler c.1904.
   Boots and shoes, which
   could not easily be made at
   home, were always a
   problem for the poorer
   families until the
   introduction of machinery,
   which brought down the
   prices considerably from the
   1870s onwards. By the 1890s
   most families were decently
   clothed and shod, bringing
   work for the cobblers whose
   dark little shops were a
   familiar feature of small
   towns and city streets.

86. 'Strawberries, all ripe
1877. John Thomson has
caught the dejection of th
street seller and his thin,
miserable pony. 'Of all
methods of obtaining
subsistence that of street
selling is the most precari
(Henry Mayhew).

▼ 87. Dancing bears (1896)
survived until after the Fi
World War, providing a
living for itinerant
showmen. One child here
dancing like the bear, whi
another watches, fascinate
A little ring of spectators i
implied by the shadows.

▶ 88. A road sweeper in
Camborne, Cornwall
c.1902. A partially
dismantled gaslamp can b
seen on the right of the
picture.

89. Fisherwomen with their
baskets of shrimps, c.1889,
Llangwm in Wales.

90. The baker not only baked bread but would often cook dinners for families who did not possess an oven. Colossal quantities of bread were eaten – a manual labourer could and did eat two pounds of bread a day with his meat and beer.

91. The kitchens of the Hotel Victoria, London in 1897. The staff seem proud of their gleaming pans and dishes, and the kitchen was electrified.

92. Shelling peas in Covent Garden c.1892. Covent Garden was a crowded, lively place: 'There is no shouting as in other markets . . . but all is bustle and confusion under the colonnade of the famous piazza.'

93. A 'sandwich man' advertising a play in one of London's numerous theatres, Terry's Theatre in the Strand. London is said to have had fifty theatres and five hundred music halls, attended by thousands of people every night. Terry's Theatre took its name from the actor Edward Terry, was opened in 1887 and later became a cinema. It was pulled down during 'improvements' to the Strand in 1923.

94. News vendor carrying placards of the Second Boer War which was to end in partial victory in 1902, perhaps Britain's first lesson that a powerful army was useless against determined guerilla resistance.

95. Dealer in fancy ware: the man who kept this stall made quite a good living, for, as he said, 'Bad as times be, it's wonderful how women will have ornaments.' The sham jewellery he sold was cheap and pretty.

96. An itinerant seller of crockery, pots and pans. Often these sellers would barter as well as take money, which may account for the group of interested women.

97. Laying wooden paving in Trafalgar Square, c.1904. Pine from Scotland and imported deal was much used for paving the streets of London, the resinous heartwood being extremely durable, thus helping to deaden the noise of traffic. But there were complaints that the wood was slippery in wet weather.

98. There was a considerable effort in the 1860s and 1870s to clear the city streets from dust, garbage and the dung of cattle and horses. This was sometimes done directly by the parish or farmed out, as here, to a 'contractor'. This water cart was the most modern kind, with an iron tank to hold the water. The driver worked from 5 am to 7 pm, spreading water to lay the dust of the summer streets. In winter he cleaned the streets.

99. Wine tasting at London Docks c.1900 – evidently a grand occasion.

Cross-cutting alder poles for clog soles (100) below. A pile of the cleft blocks from the poles can be seen in the background. The wood was green during these early stages and it was hard work for the cutters. (101) *right:* the cutter stacked the cut soles in beehive-shaped heaps to season; later the clog maker would finish the clogs. The cutters travelled the countryside in bands, often sleeping out in tents.

▼ 102. Baiting the lines, Staithes, Yorkshire, c.1905. Staithes remains a fishing village to this day.

103. A bodger, seen in the beechwoods of the Chilterns in Buckinghamshire, would turn a chair leg by hand on the pole lathe set up in his roughly made hovel.

104. Mending nets at Looe in Cornwall. One man strained the net so that the other could repair it evenly without bagging or puckering. The hobnailed boots would not have been permitted at sea, for they ruined wooden decks and were slippery and dangerou they, and the ancient shore-going bowler, would only have been worn on land.

In Town

105. Enamelled advertising signs in Carnforth, c.1898. To the modern eye Victorian advertisements seem to be one of the most attractive features of townscapes at that time.

▶ 106. Penryn, Cornwall, an attractive little town near Falmouth, built of the local granite and slate, looks very much the same today. Note the horse-droppings lying in the street, a very common hazard for Victorian pedestrians.

▶ 107. Maidstone c.1894 – The muddy street shows clearly in this photograph. No wonder mud scrapers were set in the walls of so many Victorian town houses.

108. Traffic was already a problem in London at the turn of the century, as this photograph of the Royal Exchange shows. The ladies on the top of the open buses had to endure the pain of the wind tugging at their hats, which were attached to their hair by hat pins – but perhaps the view was worth it. Meanwhile, a policeman directs the traffic and, by the lamp-post, lovers embrace apparently unconcerned by the bustle around them.

▶110. W. Highfield's Dining
and Supper Room in
London, 1904, offered a cut
from the joint for 6d, stewed
eels, jellied eels and tripe and
onions. Highfield was
obviously successful, having
another establishment off
Berwick Street in Soho. The
food seems cheap, but at this
time thirty shillings a week
was a high wage.

▼109. This cook shop, c.1870,
owned by a Mr Baylis, in
Drury Lane, was a place
where discharged convicts
could stay on their release
from prison. No convict
appeared in the photograph
lest he should be recognized
and be refused a job. The
Indian was a local character
known as Ramo Sammy, the
tam–tam man.

▶111. The Devon & Somerset
Stores c.1904, an example of
a 'chain store', with branches
in Taunton and Exeter, and a
use of repetitive placards
which has a modern look.
Brand names, familiar from
large-scale advertising in the
new-style popular press (for
instance *Daily Mail* and
Answers) were much in
evidence.

112. This village shop at Croydon c.1888 was a far cry from the modern Devon & Somerset Stores (111). It dealt in more or less anything and Austin Warner even declared himself a Cow Keeper. On display were potatoes, turnips, runner beans, cabbages, cauliflowers and tomatoes. Inhabitants of present-day Croydon would find this scene unrecognizable.

113. A fine row of shops and shoppers in Shepton Mallet. Ready-made clothing hangs outside at a safe height, the Dairy Utensil Manufactory advertises its presence by an enormous kettle sign, and beyond it a boot and shoe shop displays its wares for all to see.

▶ 114. Eastgate Street, Chester still has its handsome Victorian clock but the electric tramway has gone. There is much fine Victorian building in Chester, in harmony with the ancient town because so many of these buildings are in the traditional black and white. The Great Western Railway dray can be clearly seen. There is a sign on the right of the picture pointing the way to the 'Free Library': these first made their appearance at the end of the nineteenth century, funded by the American, Andrew Carnegie.

▶ 115. Barrow-in-Furness. A Victorian new town, Barrow owed its existence to the coming of the railway. Barrow Corporation, founded in 1867, met at first in the railway's offices before the Town Hall was built. In this photograph, taken about 1899, Barrow was complete with statues, tramlines, smoking chimneys and gothic spires, pubs and plumbers, mean streets and squalid houses. One of the founding fathers was George Ramsden, appointed Locomotive Superintendent of the Furness Railway in 1846; his name was commemorated in Ramsden Square in the town centre.

116. The imposing Wesleyan Chapel in Linthorpe Road, Middlesbrough, c.1898 – Middlesbrough was another Victorian new town and the most remarkable. In 1831 the population was 154 inhabitants. Some enterprising Quakers in 1829 bought and developed the land to export coal; later came the far more important iron industry. The Wesleyans built their first chapel in 1841. At the time of this photograph the population was about 80,000. The town was full of immigrants from all over Britain and even from the Colonies and America. At this chapel Henry Bolckow, a German, worshipped. He was a pioneer ironmaster and the first Mayor. The congregation of the Wesleyan Methodists were largely the middle classes and the 'respectable' working classes.

117. Liverpool c.1880. A bustling scene witnesses th[e] vigour of nineteenth-centu[ry] Liverpool with its teeming population. In 1884, the density of population in some parts of the city was 1,200 to an acre. Its export[s] exceeded London's; its poverty probably likewise. In the 1860s Taine describe[d] the Irish quarter of Liverpo[ol] as 'the nethermost circle of hell'. In the 1850s, only 45 per cent of babies born in t[he] city reached the age of twenty. In the 1880s and 1890s infant mortality was still extremely high, and th[e] population over the age of was small. These figures gi[ve] a sinister meaning to Sykes Family Mourning Establishment which can b[e] seen on the right of the picture.

118. Piccadilly, Manchest[er] – 1886. By this time Manchester was no longer just a mushroom city of cotton mills. It had becom[e a] great provincial capital. Waterhouse's Town Hall, adorned by Ford Madox Brown frescoes, the new University and the Hallé Orchestra were all signs of concern with culture and intellect.

119. Traffic in Trafalgar
Square, c.1905. A Borwick's
horse-drawn bus can be seen
to the right of the picture.
Borwick's were one of the
many bus operators in
London.

120. Church Street, Blackpool – c.1905. By now workmen could reasonably expect a Saturday half holiday as well as a free Sunday. Excursions to Blackpool from industrial Lancashire became the rule and the workman had money to spend on his amusements. Music hall was popular while the Palace offered the delights of Winter Gardens and a Ballroom.

122. Taunton in 1903. 'The prevailing impression Taunton gives is that of a clean-looking modern town: which, by the way, was the very first in England to adopt electric lighting' . . . as a guide book of 1894 described it, adding that it was 'much frequented by the country people.' Trams run through the main street.

121. The motor vehicle begins to make its presence felt (in 1901 there were 8,000 cars in Britain). In Buckham High Street, c.1906, there were already garages on both sides of the street.

123. Bideford, Devon, c.1906. Once a thriving po[rt] Bideford was a sleepy cou[ntry] town. A rider leading a packhorse, a man prepari[ng] to mount a bicycle, little g[irls] in broad-brimmed hats riding in a pony cart were [the] only traffic in the High St[reet] which might have been he[ld] up by the wagon position[ed] right across the road.

124. Braintree, Essex. A policeman stands impressively outside 'The People's Bootmaker' (righ[t]) keeping an eye on quantiti[es] of children.

125. Great Yarmouth – Row
112, c.1891. A last glimpse of
the medieval town; the Rows
were narrow alleys, dating
from the thirteenth century,
where lived the fishermen of
the herring fleet and less
well-to-do traders. 40,000
people lived in the 150 rows.

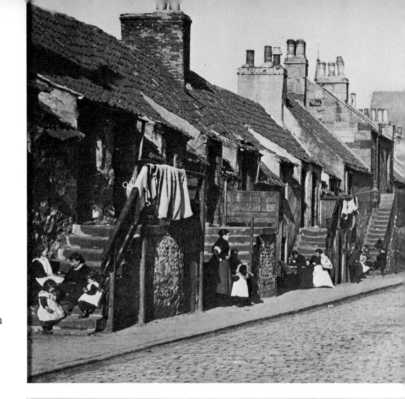

126. Edinburgh – fishermen's cottages at Newhaven c.1899, with masts of sailing ships in the background. In poor weather, when the children could not play on the steps, the poky, dilapidated cottages must have been cramped and depressing for the large families who lived there.

127. Boston, Lincolnshire in 1888 with a sailing boat moored at a warehouse on the River Witham. The harbour and channel were deepened and enlarged towards the end of the nineteenth century in an attempt to stop the gradual decay of the ancient port.

128. White Hind Alley, Bankside in 1896. 'A noticeable thing in poor streets is the mark left on the exterior of the houses. All along the front, about on a level with the hips, there is a broad dirty mark, showing where the men and lads are in the constant habit of standing . . .' (*Life and Labour of the People in London* – edited by Charles Booth.) This testimony of unemployment is very clear in the photograph.

129. Moss Alley, Bankside c.1896. 'The men have a good time compared to the women, who lead fearfully hard and slavish lives . . .' city vicar writing in the 1890s.

130. Lister Gate, Nottingham c.1887. Nottingham prospered fro[m] its machine-made lace and stockings. Its five-acre market place was covered [on] Saturdays with booths and stalls and the celebrated Goose Fair was held there [for] 400 years until the buildin[g] of the vast new Council House in 1928 removed th[e] Fair to the Forest Recreati[on] Ground, where it now tak[es] place during the first week [of] October. Boots, the Chemists, was started in Goose Gate as a one-man business.

131. Norwich – The Arc[ade] c.1901. Even at this time photographers were sufficiently rare that peop[le] watched them curiously – and were very willing to pose for them.

132. King Edward Street, Hull, in 1903. The old town was more or less demolished by bombing during the Second World War. The picture shows the tramlines in the centre of the road, the cupolas of the dock offices and the monument to Wilberforce, 'The nightingale of the House of Commons', whose efforts led to the 1833 Act abolishing slavery throughout the Empire.

133. Jamaica Street, Glasgow, c.1896. Activity in Glasgow city streets was as great as in any of the English cities like London and Manchester.

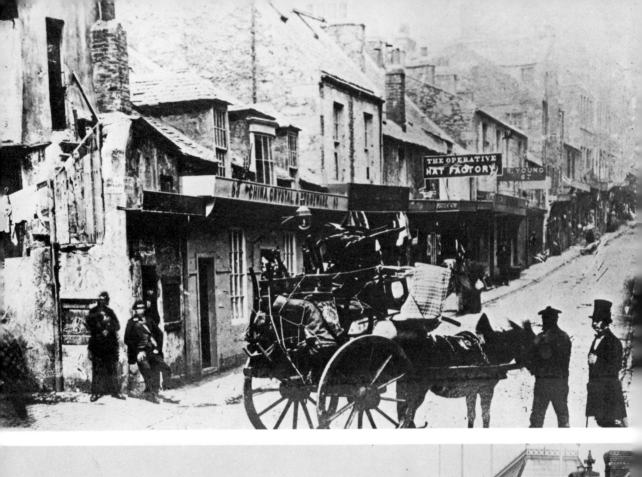

◀ 134. By comparison with Jamaica Street (133), this Edinburgh street in the 1860s had the look of a medieval city.

◀135. Victoria Street, Belfast's city centre c.1900. There is noticeably less bustle here than in contemporary photographs of other British city centres. Most of the traffic was little donkey carts.

▲136. St Mary's Street, Cardiff, c.1899. A formal group of staff outside the Great Western Hotel.

Country Matters

137. A farmer and his wife grinding corn on the Isle of Skye.

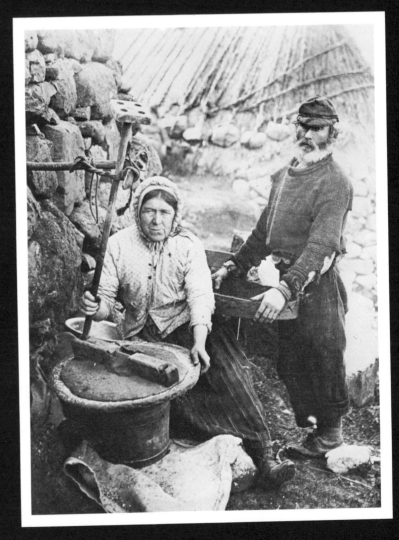

The reaper-binder (138) was
evolved on the vast
wheatfields of the American
Middle West at the turn of
the century and did away
with the army of labourers
who had gathered the cut
corn and tied it with sheaves;
here the machine is followed
only by one small boy in
boater and Eton collar. (139):
the sheaves being stood in
stooks or shocks to dry out
before being stacked.
Threshing was not done until
the winter.

▶ 140. Tea in the hayfield. Note the colossal mugs.

▼ 141. The really skilled part of the hay making was loading the hay wain evenly, so that the load would not slip. It must have been hot work for the woman – perhaps the farmer's wife – in her tight bodice and heavy skirt.

142. Mowing at Netherbury in Dorset.

144. Carting logs from the churchyard at Ockley, Surrey, c.1903.

143. The Victorian country scene at its best – bringing home the hay, c.1910, along the hot, dusty track. Wire netting had now made its appearance, although iron and wooden fences were still widely used.

146. Dipping sheep in 1902. This was made compulsory in 1905. This little galvanized bath would have been used only for very small flocks; larger flocks had big swim-through dips.

145. Sheep shearing was very hard work. A large jar, probably of ginger beer, awaits the thirsty shearers, in a bucket of water to keep it cool. The rolled-up fleeces were packed into wool sacks and a man can be seen treading them down.

147. A team of oxen with their driver, c.1900, probably in Sussex. Oxen continued to be used as draught animals well into the twentieth century. Many Sussex farmers preferred them to horses for they were dual-purpose animals; they were worked from the age of three years to six or seven, when they were rested, fattened and sent to the butcher. An ox could pull a heavy load fifteen miles a day, and on one occasion a Sussex ox completed the four-mile Lewes race-course in sixteen minutes.

148. Jimmy Macmillan exhibited Herefords for Queen Victoria and King Edward VII for many years, winning several Championships at Royal Shows. Here he is with Admiral, a big winner at the Royal Kent Show in 1908.

149. The new age in agriculture: Crawley Fair in Sussex, the market place cluttered with cattle driven in to be sold and dominated by an elevator, which looks gigantic compared to the small-scale buildings. They were used to pitch corn (in sheaves), hay and straw on to a stack, and farmers thought that they kept the men better tempered than when the heaving was done manually. Some workers, however, disliked the relentless pace of the machine and the dust that was thrown out. Elevators were powered by wheel, turned either by horse or by steam. At this date (c.1905) most big farmers possessed an elevator.

▲ 150. The cattle market at Llanrwst in Gwynedd, North Wales, c.1896, was typical of the many small weekly markets in country towns that had largely replaced the old, big fairs by this time. Dealers came to buy the cattle in twos and threes from small farmers, who could at the same time buy supplies of corn or seed from the covered exchanges which existed in almost all country market towns.

▲ 152. Guisborough in Yorkshire's North Riding is still a market town; the picture shows the market place, c.1908; the grocer sold the famous Yorkshire hams and bacon. The cobbles still survive.

◄151. Okehampton, Devon, c.1890: market day in this little town, high in Dartmoor. When the poet Gerard Manley Hopkins visited the Moor he walked 'by starlight and Jupiter, stumbling down steep, dark lanes'; now it would be in the glare of headlights from holiday traffic.

153. A blind beggar at a cattle market, photographed in 1894 by Paul Martin, probably in Devon.

154. Pony sale, New Forest, c.1905. The New Forest ponies are famou their stamina, being abl carry a man weighing te eleven stone all day whi rounded up the wild po which remained all the y in the forest without ha feeding. Regulations for preserving and improvi the breed have existed si 1885.

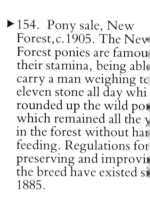

155. Saddlers Row, Petworth, Sussex in 1905. Petworth, a large village, could support specialist shops. The newsagent then, as now, sold tobaccos and stationery; a saddler and harness maker had been in the same street, judging by its name, probably since Tudor times.

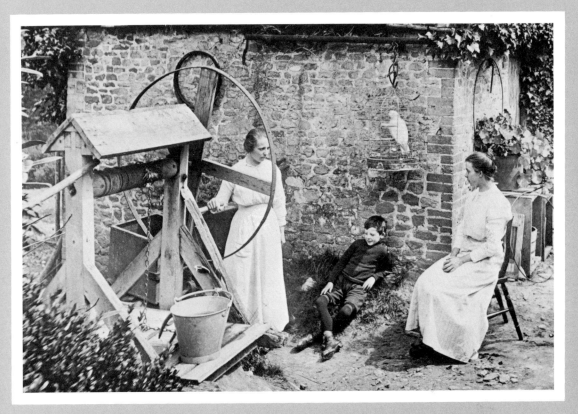

157. Drawing the water, 1900. Country houses, small and large, had no mains water and a filter was an essential household item, right up until the 1930s. Giant earthenware pillars, they were supposed to make the water palatable and safe to drink.

156. Fetching water. Even in the cities it was common to have no running water until well into this century. The water from wells, brooks and rivers in the country was often muddy and foul-smelling.

Sudbury mill, Suffolk.
bury, birthplace of
nsborough, was an
ortant market town from
ent times. The splendid
on the River Stour
ed a large agricultural
and was a comparatively
cient and modern affair.

▲ 160. The country postman
brings letters to the Blue Ball
Inn at Countisbury, Devon,
c.1907. Charles Booth
considered 'the letter written
home by the country girl
settled in domestic service in
the great town' was 'one of
the most powerful and
efficient migration agencies'
(*Life and Labour in London*,
1902). The penny post meant
letters could be sent cheaply;
the Education Act of 1870
brought literacy to
thousands, enabling them to
use the cheap postal service.

◀159. Kentish watermill, still
in use c.1910, probably for
grinding animal feedstuffs.

The Loxhill Post
[Offic]e, c.1905, was also the
[groc]ery and the bakery. The
[postm]istress and the
[teleg]ram boy stand outside.

The forge at Merrow:
[the h]orseshoe arch can also
[be se]en at forges such as the
[one a]t Penshurst, Kent (now
[a gara]ge).

A blacksmith in his
[forge] – not an ordinary
[villa]ge forge, possibly one
[attac]hed to a factory.

164. A two-waggon gypsy family in their working clothes, with seven children glaring at the camera. The beautiful caravans were in common use at least until the 1950s. Mayhew wrote of 'the nomadic races of England', 'In each of the classes above-mentioned, there is a greater development of the animal than of the intellectual or moral nature of man, and they are all more or less distinguished for their high cheek-bones and protruding jaws – for their use of a slang language – for their lax ideas of property – for their general improvidence – for their repugnance to continuous labour – their disregard of female honour – their love of cruelty – their pugnacity – and their utter want of religion.'

Charcoal burners, c.1900. The charcoal was made in the woods, as the wood was heavy to transport while the charcoal was light. A chimney of split logs was arranged around a central stake. The other logs, left in the round, were carefully stacked in layers around the chimney to form a dome shape about fifteen feet in diameter at the base. The dome was then covered with some such material as straw, bracken or leaves; finally the whole was covered with earth or ashes to exclude the air. The heap was then lit by dropping burning charcoal down the chimney and adding some dry wood. Once the stack was alight the flue was sealed and the charcoal burner watched and tended it for the two to ten days necessary for the burning, meanwhile preparing another stack. The brushwood screen around the heap protected it from side draughts which would make it burn unevenly or too fast. (165 and 166)

167. Charcoal burner's hut:
these crudely made cabins
were later replaced by huts or
caravans.

168. Woodcutters at
Lostwithiel in Cornwall,
c.1900, on the road to
Restormel Castle. The
brushwood was valued as
faggots providing a quick
blaze for home cooking and
for bakeries; slightly thick
rods were trimmed with
bill hook and used for
staking plants. Nowadays
forest workers generally
burn the brushwood; it is
bulky to be transported
economically.

169. The pond at Chertsey in Surrey, c.1904. The carter had driven into the pond, not just to allow his horse to have a drink, but to tighten up his cart wheels by swelling the damp wood.

170. A coracle man. The Towy estuary near Carmarthen was once covered with these odd-looking one-man boats, used for fishing. There is said to be a ghost which crosses the Taf in a coracle, at nearby Laugharne Castle. Coracles have survived until present times on the river Teifi in Cardiganshire.

171. This early milk bar seems to have served milk straight from the cow – as well as sweets and aerated waters.

172. A milk delivery cart, c.1895 at Downderry in Cornwall. The dairy woman covered the milk cans with a cloth to keep off the dust from the road. Alerted by the donkey's bell, the customer had her money ready.

◄173. Two washerwomen.

►174. Plucking a goose in 1904. The feathers were kept for bedding.

▼175. Brick making, c.1888, probably in Essex. The brick maker is shaping lumps of puddled clay in a wooden brick mould. Two shaped bricks can be seen on the ledge behind him, each on its board to be stacked to dry. His mate is stacking the shaped bricks on to a barrow. A pile of boards stand ready to receive the bricks. After drying, the bricks were fired in kilns and these old kilns can still be found all over the clay areas of the south-east, usually in stands of coppice which were used for fuel.

▼176. Sharpening a bagging
hook at the communal
grindstone, Suffolk. These
grindstones were a familiar
sight in large gardens and
village workshops before
verge-cutting machinery and
small grass cutters came into
common use in the 1950s.
The boy is turning the handle
so that the man can sharpen
his blade. A refinement was
to have a stone turned by a
treadle.

▶177. Paul Martin's
photograph of a tramp, 1
'I rigged up my camera a
exposed three plates. He
took no notice. I gave hi▮
shilling; but still he rema▮
silent.'

178. A gardener in London in the 1870s. A grape vine like the one in this glass house was the pride of many Victorian gardeners; they were also fond of growing pineapples, known confusingly as 'pines'.

179. The market gardener, Suffolk. This operation look very small-scale, but many large farmers, ruined by cheap imported ham and wheat, had had to turn to producing vegetables in the 1870s and later.

10. A countryman's
dinner, c.1900 – a
well-earned break from
hedging and ditching.

11. Carrying the morning
milk at Broom Squires
Cottage, Hindhead, Surrey,
1907.

12. A hill shepherd.

Hop pickers in East
, c.1901. This was the
tional holiday for
lon's poor until the
ines took over as late as
950s. These pickers look
ough they are enjoying
selves although the
usually went on from
n to dusk.

▼184. Making lace in the
1890s. The lace makers were
hit hard by the invention of
lace-making machines, but
part of the traditional cottage
industry survived. They
were much helped by the
patronage of Queen Victoria
who loved lace (her wedding
dress had been made of it).

▲185. Cave dwellers of the
1890s at Downderry Cave.

186. High Salvington Mill, c.1914. This mill like so many others was a casualty of the decline of British agriculture. Wheat, largely imported, was milled in large flour mills using the roller process, in the larger ports such as London and Liverpool, and the little local mills with their traditional millstones, were used chiefly for gristing – milling coarse grains for animal food. In 1879 there were still 10,000 mills making flour in Britain, but by the end of the century the number had fallen to less than 1,000, nearly all of which were roller mills. At High Salvington Mill the broken-down fence and the troop of sightseers betray the lack of activity.

Getting Around

187. Bowness Ferry c.1897. Bowness pier is the ferry centre of Lake Windermere to this day. This ferry is transporting a man and cart across the lake and a ferry is still used by motorists to avoid the long trip around the lake. Even in the 1890s Bowness was a favourite place for yachting and fishing holidays.

188. The pier at Douglas, Isle of Man, c.1903. The island was even more of a foreign country at this date than at present, with over 4,000 people able to speak the Manx language.

▼189. Landing stage, Wallasey receiving room no.2, Woodside receiving room no.3, Liverpool c.1894. The Mersey Tunnel has now removed most of the *raison d'être* for the ferries which used to bustle to and fro over the Mersey, but the ferry still crosses from Liverpool to the pleasant resort of Wallasey, and takes only seven minutes. The Woodside ferry has a long history; probably back before Birkenhead Priory was established in the twelfth century. The steam ferry from Liverpool began to operate in 1817 and this new accessibility encouraged the growth of Birkenhead from a small village into a ship-building port.

190. Barry docks c.1899: steam and sail side by side.

▲ 191. A floating bridge at Cowes, c.1913. This replaced the old ferryman, who used to take passengers across in his small rowing boat.

▶ 192. Loading bundles of poles on to the barge, *Perseverance*, needed a footsure bargee to bring the loads along the planks and trestles to the loader in the barge, while the family waited and the thin horse enjoyed the rest. The barge, based at Brentford in Middlesex, operated in the Thames Waterway between London and Reading.

193. Waiting for the boat to
come through the lock,
c.1902. The semi-diesel
engine came into general use
from about 1911, although
steam was being used
experimentally from the
1800s on steam tugs.
Horse-drawn, narrow boats
could take a load of up to
thirty tons.

194. Underground railway, London 1860s. Designed to connect the main line station termini in London, the railway was not strictly underground initially but was built mostly in cuttings just below street level which were later arched over, thus slicing through the network of sewers, gas and water mains and cables that was by then the substructure of all great cities. This method was used in the Metropolitan and District Lines but was extremely expensive and the steam engines made the atmosphere unpleasant; later, in the 1880s, deep-level tunnelling coincided with electricity to make it possible to open the first deep-level railway in the world, the first section being the City and South London Railway between the Bank and Stockwell.

195. Liverpool railway station, c. 1870: at this date the engine crews had very little protection from the weather. The engineman on the right, in his white corduroys, would have collected many smuts before the journey was over. When protective windscreens and rudimentary cabs were introduced, the hardy enginemen resisted them, saying they would obstruct their view ahead and it was not until the 1880s that roofed-over cabs with large windows were introduced.

▲197. The mountain railway on Snowdon. The Victorians 'discovered' mountains and a cogged rail to the summit of Snowdon paid its way. Off the picture was probably a ladies' carriage – certainly no ladies are to be seen in this picture.

◄196. The Jersey railway in 1898, and Gorey with Mont Orgueil Castle in the background. There is no rail service now in Jersey.

198. Traffic on Tower Bridge c.1900. Vegetables going into London, passengers coming out. Tower Bridge had been completed in 1894 – the work of engineer Sir John Wolfe-Barry – and was made to look like a medieval drawbridge by architect Horace Jones.

199. A delivery van passing through the Dulwich tollgate, c.1910. The tollgate in College Road, which leads to Crystal Palace, is the last to operate in London.

200. A policeman directing London traffic.

201. A tram in Tyrrel Street, Bradford, c.1903. The first trams were horse-drawn, then they were drawn by steam – but neither was satisfactory. Electricity was first used in Blackpool, from an electrified rail; in Leeds in 1891 an overhead wire provided current and this became the standard system.

▲ 202. Ightham, Kent in 1901: milk is being delivered to the 'Commercial and Bicycle Hotel'. The miller has perhaps called in at 'The Railway Bell', where P. Brook was the proprietor.

▶ 203. The funicular railway at Bridgnorth, Shropshire, c.1902. Bridgnorth is built partly above red sandstone cliffs, partly at their foot. This railway must have been a boon to the inhabitants, for the climb to High Town from Low Town was up very steep flights of steps.

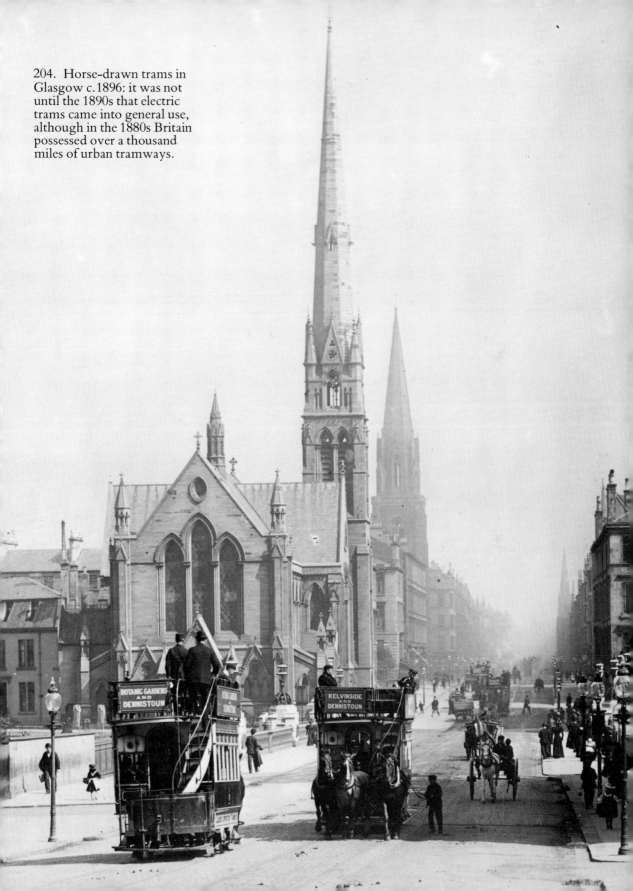

204. Horse-drawn trams in Glasgow c.1896: it was not until the 1890s that electric trams came into general use, although in the 1880s Britain possessed over a thousand miles of urban tramways.

205. Motor charabanc at Hindhead, c.1905. The grim-looking passengers were presumably bent on pleasure, for Hindhead was then, as now, one of the chief beauty spots of south-east England and charabancs were just coming into their own, immortalized by A.D. Godley's donnish jingle which begins: 'What is this that roareth thus? Can it be a Motor Bus? Yes, the smell and hideous hum, Indicat Motorem Bum.'

▲ 206. The Red Lion Hotel, Handcross, Sussex, early this century. Bread and butter tea is advertised for 6d. The occupants of the bus from Brighton with its open top and the open cars, with their straw hatted passengers must have been quite wet. The driver of the second car has blurred the negative in his hurry to get under cover.

► 208. The cyclist's rest, c.1910, at 'The Old Oak Tree', Cobham in Surrey. 'The Old Oak Tree' was obviously a favourite for children and the enterprising proprietor catered also for passing motorists.

207. The Haslemere-Hindhead-Grayshott motorbus at the Royal Huts Hotel, which offered Good Stabling as well as petrol and oil, c.1910.

209. *Inset* The puncture c.1910. Games and pastimes were often taken on early motor expeditions to while away the time spent on the inevitable repairs. It is clear from the raised umbrella that a lady inside the car is protecting herself from the sun.

210. The Cat and Fiddle, Buxton, Derbyshire. By the time this picture was taken in 1913, motor transport was quite common. Note the basket-work sidecar on the motor bike, the two spare tyres on the car and the comfortable-looking Daimler bus.

211. The Guildford coach about to leave the Angel Hotel, c.1895.

▲212. An outing about 1855.
Probably the crinolined
mother and daughter were
going to pay calls on friends.
A *Punch* cartoon of the time
showed an enormously
skirted lady about to enter a
small carriage.
Impudent boy: 'I say, Bill!
Come and see the conjuring
– Here's this here gal a goin'
to squeeze herself into that
there broom!' This lady takes
up all the front seat while her
daughter perches behind.

▶213. Riding an ordinary, or
pennyfarthing, in Deansgate,
Manchester in the 1880s.
'The position, so nicely
balanced, nearly on one
wheel; the absence of a wheel
to be pushed in front,
wheelbarrow fashion; the
free, billowy rolling motion
that ensued, gave to riding
and coasting on it a peculiar
charm that was wholly its
own, and afforded sensations
which those who have
enjoyed them count as
among the most beautiful of
their lives,' wrote an
enthusiast in the 1880s.

▲ 215. The coach is about to
leave the Blue Ball Inn,
Countisbury, Devon,
c.1907. The little-used coach
roads were considered
expensive anachronisms in
the railway age, rather as the
railways are today. Soon
motorcars and buses were to
take over the roads and push
the railways into second
place.

214. The Philpott delivery van c.1898 – Philpotts were manufacturers of aerated waters. The bottles were sealed with a glass marble, held in place by the pressure; to open them, the marble was pressed down into the bottle. Later, when the bottles were returned to the manufacturer, jets of water were used to expel the marble from the bottle. The marbles were carried away in the water and children would delight in diving in to fish them out.

216. Brook's Packhorse Co., Burnham, c.1887. A four-wheeler and two gigs outside the stables; the ostler stands in the archway.

217. Bath chairs at Bath,
c.1907. The attendants seem
to be vying with each other
for the superiority of their
steering handles at the
entrance to the Great Roman
Bath.

218. The bath chair was pushed from behind and could be steered by the occupant; it had a flap over the knees and a hood which could be drawn up if it rained. Bath chairs were cumbersome things; whoever pushed this lady must have found it hard work.

220. Hydraulic lift, Lynton, Devon c.1896. The Cliff Railway between Lynton and Lynmouth, which is almost directly below Lynton, still functions. It was founded by George Newnes, the publisher, in 1890, and works like a pair of scales; the car going down is weighted with water and pulls the other up to the top.

219. Taking to the air by balloon from a London gasworks, c.1910. The motto on the balloon's side, 'Dolce Far Niente', seems particularly apt. Balloons, a French invention, were regarded with scorn in Britain, as indeed were the early attempts to build heavier-than-air flying machines, and Frederick Lanchester's experiments in this country in the 1890s were ignored by his countrymen though they aroused interest in Germany.

221. An old man and a boy
resting outside the 'Pilchards
Inn', Polperro, Cornwall
c.1910. The inn was named
after the fish which were
such an important part of the
Cornish fishermen's
livelihood.

222. Dancing to the organ in
Lambeth in the 1890s. 'In the
streets, many a moment of
quiet enjoyment has been
afforded to the tired artisan
by these modern minstrels.'

Time Off

▲ 223. A servant in a
gentleman's club caught
off-duty with the 'Grand
Trunk Railway System'
time-tables.

▶ 224. Playing cards c. 1900 –
with plenty of liquid
refreshment.

'It is no wonder that boating combining as it does amusement with healthy exercise, should find increasing favour among these hardy damsels who do not fear to win enjoyment at the expense of bodily exertion.' No wonder indeed, for mixed boating parties must have been a welcome change from the formalities of drawing room evenings looking at albums and listening to tinkling pianos. A pleasant day out at Surbiton (225) previous page; eager spectators at Worcester regatta (226); and Regatta Day at Moulsey Lock (227).

228. A pleasure cruise on a paddle steamer at Totnes in Devon, c.1896 – 'In the last century the highlight of the summer for thousands of people' (Hugh McKnight). If no steamer was available a working boat would be hired, packed with benches and bottles of lemonade, and used for school and charity outings.

229. Feeding the swans in a public park in Taunton, c.1906. Public parks were more or less unheard of before the 1840s and in the 1880s a Nonconformist minister, Robert Dale, was campaigning for them in Birmingham as part of a municipal policy 'which lessened the miseries of the wretched and added brightness to the life of the desolate'.

230. Box Hill on a Bank Holiday, c.1906. Statutory Bank Holidays, four every year, started in 1871. Workers would pour out of the cities on August Monday in brakes and, later, charabancs, often to the disgust of the puritanical. 'Very rarely does one hear a good word for the Bank Holidays. The more common view is that they are a curse.'

◄231. The Proposal, c.1888.
A somewhat amateurish
example of a posed
photograph in the manner of
the paintings popular at the
time. Though scorned by the
élite, these photographs
found their way on to the
walls of many Victorian
homes.

▲232. A young lady rowing
in the 1890s. Wasp waists of
twenty-two inches were *de
rigueur* and girls were put
into stays from the age of
thirteen.

▶ 233. The Thames at
Marlow, 1887; the
photographer waiting for a
photograph.

▶ 234. Beach photographer,
Southend Marine Parade
c.1892. Itinerant
photographers travelled
from the towns when
business was slack to find
clients at racecourses, seaside
and holiday resorts.

▶ 235. Bathing machines for
gentlemen, Hastings c.1888.
'Brief directions for
sea-bathing. 1. Take the cold
sponge bath before breakfast.
2. Five or ten minutes walk
before sitting down to that
meal. 3. Eat sparingly. 4.
Bathe in the sea two hours
after breakfast. 5. Keep
moving about while in the
water. 6. Do not stop in over
five minutes the first day,
and never over ten unless
you are strong and can swim.
7. Rub well down and dress;
saunter homewards, and if
hungry take a cup of
cocoatina, a tiny biscuit and
afterwards forty winks if
required.'

▲ 236. Yarmouth sands. In 1892 Paul Martin took a holiday at Yarmouth with his 'Improved Facile' came adapted by himself. 'It is impossible to describe the thrill which taking the firs snaps without being notic gave one,' he wrote, and took several photographs working-class couples spooning on the beach as they waited for the 'Conc Party' to begin.

◄ 237. Hastings in the 188C In order to protect their dresses from sand and mu ladies sewed yards of 'bru braid' around the hems or their skirts; when they ca into the house they, or th maids, would spend a go hour or so brushing away dirt.

238. Southend's renowned pier, c.1892, still the longest in the world, at the height of its glory.

239. A beach party at Hastings in 1864 from Frith's *The Gossiping Photographer at Hastings*, a travelogue written, photographed and published by himself.

240. The band stand at Deal: a popular concert by a brass band, c.1906, surrounded by prams, bicycles, bath chairs, schoolboys and parasoled ladies.

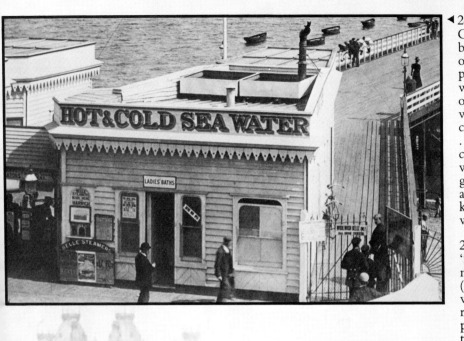

241. The ladies' baths at Clacton-on-Sea, c.1895. Sea bathing was considered a bit of an ordeal and many preferred the salt water baths where the water could be hot or cold. 'If you are anywhere where hot salt water baths can be had, go in for a course . . . they are delightfully calming and toning to the whole system. They induce gentle sleep and improve the appetite, while they ease all kinds of chronic pains,' wrote a doctor in 1897.

242. Scarborough, c.1891. 'Scarborough, the fair mistress of that coast' (Census of 1871). The watering-places and seaside resorts increased their population at a faster rate than almost any other towns in Britain. Scarborough was known as 'The Queen of northern watering-places.' Parasols are in evidence as shade from the sun.

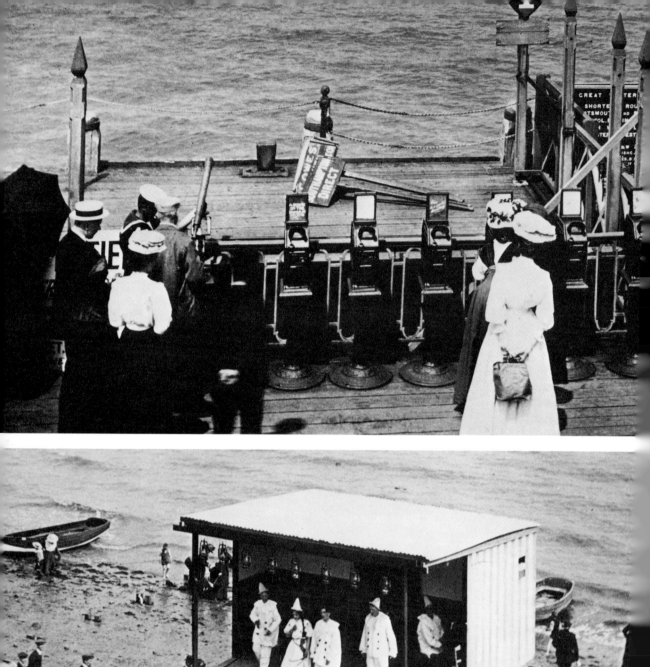
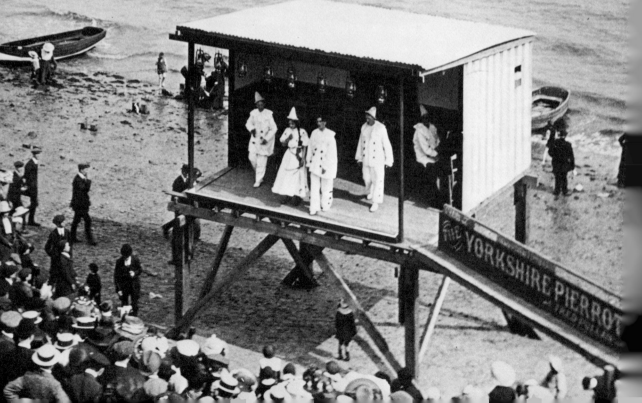

◀ 244. The beach attraction at Clacton-on-Sea, c.1912, of 'The Yorkshire Pierrots and Fred Pullin'. The original Pierrot was a solitary, pathetic, clownish character, but following a highly successful, mimed Pierrot play, 'L'enfant prodigue' in London in 1891, Pierrot troupes began to appear all over England on beaches and in pier pavilions, taking the place of the 'nigger minstrels'. They would put on various entertainments such as conjuring, juggling and singing.

▲ 245. Blackpool c.1876. Most of the buildings in the photograph have disappeared, except for the pier and the famous tower, up which a lift carries sightseers to admire the view from the top, 518 feet above the ground. The *Encore*, a pleasure boat, makes out to sea.

246. The pier at Beaumaris in North Wales c.1897. The ladies are well wrapped up and clinging to their hats; the Bulkeley Arms Hotel is operating today.

247. The lighthouse at New Brighton near Liverpool, c.1886. Ferries still ply between Liverpool and New Brighton bringing Liverpudlians to enjoy the resort with its pleasure cruises and views of the Mersey. Eager sightseers can be seen ascending the lighthouse by its ladder.

▼ 248. Meeting an acquaintance on the esplanade, Fleetwood, c.1892.

▲ 249. Sandown Parade (Isle of Wight) c.1908. Promenade and parades were a great feature of Victorian resorts, presumably for the brief walks considered so essential before and after bathing. When meeting an acquaintance for the second time it was not necessary to bow once more. 'Should your eyes meet, a slight smile of recognition would suffice.'

◀ 250. The Ferris Wheel at Blackpool, c.1897, sadly no longer exists. Its statistics were impressive; thirty cars, each of which could hold thirty people, weight 1,000 tons, height 220 feet. It operated from its erection in 1896 until 1928, when it was broken up for scrap.

▲ 251. Ladies were expected to play musical instruments and sing. Some of the warnings given in etiquette books of the time suggest that the performances were frequently painful.

▶ 252. The Lyceum Theatre: the Sunday queue c.1903. The crowd was queuing to see *Hamlet* with Matheson Lang, cousin to Cosmo Lang, the late Archbishop of Canterbury. Matheson had been destined for the Church, but became a famous actor. The Lyceum's great period was from 1878 to 1902, when, under Irving's control, it was one of London's foremost theatres; a brief period of music hall followed; from 1907-9 it once more produced Shakespeare, other drama and pantomime. In 1909 it was taken over by the eccentric Melville brothers and launched into highly successful pantomime and melodrama. The 1834 building was scheduled for demolition in 1939, but was saved by the outbreak of war and is now a dance hall.

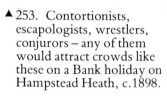

▲ 253. Contortionists,
escapologists, wrestlers,
conjurors – any of them
would attract crowds like
these on a Bank holiday on
Hampstead Heath, c.1898.

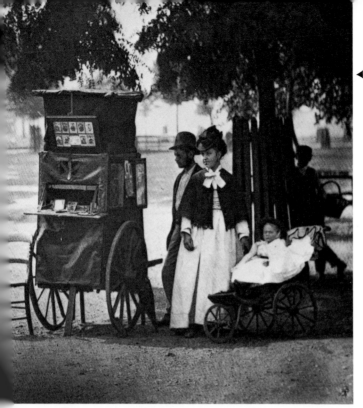

254. A photographer on Clapham Common in 1877. Nursemaid and baby posed for their picture. Nursemaids were the photographer's best clients, for they would recommend him to the other nursemaids they met and the proud mother, when shown the picture, would also recommend him to her friends.

255. The Sunday painter, probably J.B. Surgey, a great friend of Francis Frith, who was himself also an accomplished painter in oils. The pair of them would often go off on painting expeditions when on holiday.

256. Crowds at the Derby
c.1913 – also often painted,
notably by William Frith
(when his 'Derby Day' was
exhibited in 1858, railings
had to be erected to protect
the picture from the crowds
who wished to see it).

257. Bicycling in the nineties. 'Now women, even young girls, ride alone or attended only by some casual man friend for miles together through deserted country roads. The danger of this is apparent, but parents and guardians will probably become wise after the event. Given a lonely road, and a tramp desperate with hunger or naturally vicious, and it stands to reason that a girl, or indeed any woman, riding alone must be in some considerable peril' (Mrs F. Harcourt Williamson, 1897).

258. In the depths of winter, when ponds and lakes froze over, skating was a popular pastime. A close-fitting dress, well clear of the ankles, was considered suitable skating wear for ladies. 'Fur is too heavy and something lighter should be worn as a covering for the head . . . a sheet of brown paper placed between the outer and the under clothing is a capital chest protector.'

'Oh, *do* skate, Mr Winkle,' said Arabella. 'I like to see it *so* much.'

'Oh, it is *so* graceful,' said another young lady. A third young lady said it was elegant, and a fourth expressed her opinion that it was 'swan-like' (*Pickwick Papers*).

259. This picture, taken about 1900, shows the Town Regatta at Maldon, Essex, with craft getting under way for the smack race which was the highlight of this event. The Regatta is still held. The sailing barge dressed overall would be the Committee Boat.

◄ Advertising Salmon's tea.
Airships and hot air balloons
are the modern equivalent of
these splendid aerial
hoardings. The elephant
(260) floats over the
Serpentine, London; the lion
(261) over a London square.

▼ 262. Believe it or not, the
contraption in the centre was
a lemonade bar c.1895.

263. Lord's Cricket Ground – home of the Marylebone Cricket Club. The crowd strolls on the sacred turf in an interval between play.

▼ 264. The putt about to sink –
a golfing match in
progress, c. 1910. The caddies
are probably the sons of the
players.

▲ 265. The staghounds meet at
Hunters Inn, Barnstaple
c. 1900.

266. The entomologist, c.1910. Harold Bastin, who took this photograph, was an entomologist and a natural history photographer; this snap may be of his brother who was involved in his business and was also an entomologist.

267. The start of the race.

Communal Spirit

269. 'The Old George', Bethnal Green in 1885. The large crowd (including the ubiquitous policeman), the staggering array of beer barrels and the line-up of workers each holding a tankard all indicate a celebration, possibly connected with the General Election of November that year.

268. A wedding group c.1910 – a time when all the family gathered together.

270. The King Edward Sanatorium at Midhurst in Kent was one of about seventy in Britain for the treatment of tuberculosis, still at this date (c.1907) a major scourge.

271. The Wayfarer's Dole at St Cross Hospital, Winchester, c.1908. The dole consists of bread and beer from a horn cup; this charity has been dispensed here since the twelfth century and is still given today.

272. Four of the customary
thirteen poor men for whom
Bishop Henry de Blois
founded the Hospital of St
Cross in Winchester in 1132.
They still wear their black
gowns decorated with a
silver cross, but instead of
those hats, they now wear a
medieval cap (c.1906).

▲ 273. Salisbury in 1895:
going to market for fruit and
vegetables. Most towns of
any size had these communal
open-air markets but those
who lived in the suburbs of
large cities had to depend on
the local greengrocer, who
would himself go in early to
the main city markets.

274. Market day at Sudbury, Suffolk c.1903; horse trading was going on as well as the sale of farm machinery.

275. A temperance parade. The middle classes on the march: 'We Drink God's Pure Beverage', c.1906. The temperance movement was especially strong in nonconformist areas of Britain, such as Wales, Lancashire, Yorkshire, East Anglia and Cornwall.

276. The full splendour of a military parade in Weymouth in 1898. The bathing machines – one for ladies, one for gentlemen – are a reminder that Weymouth owed its prestige as a resort to the use there of the very first bathing machine in 1763. George III came to try it out in 1789 to the strains of the National Anthem and paid several more visits, staying in the Gloucester Hotel, which can be seen on the right. Most of the buildings on the sea front remain today.

277. A self-righting lifeboat with its life-jacketed crew, at Tenby, c.1891. The lifeboat service was, and still is, voluntary and manned chiefly by fishermen whose wives would come down to help launch the heavy boats at any time and in any weather.

▲ 279. The village postman confronts the sailor home from sea, a familiar figure in the traditionally sea-faring parts of the country. This photograph was taken at Lostwithiel in Cornwall.

◄ 278. Flamborough Head, Yorkshire, where fishermen still haul up their cobbles and unload their crab pots under the steep chalk cliffs.

POST OFFICE

▲ 280. The Post Office at Camborne in Cornwall – rather a large establishment, as Camborne was the heart of Cornwall's mining country. A photographer was a rare enough sight even by the turn of the century for women to watch from the windows.

▶ 281. The village postman handing a letter to a hedger, c.1912. The postal service reached out by this date into both town and country.

▲282. City of Westminster
dustcart c.1898. 'In the
winter the oozy, jammy mud
sloshed about, and the street
cleaners scraped it up in
delicious soupy spoonfuls
and threw it into their carts.
And everywhere and all the
time there was the smell of
horses . . .' (Gwen Raverat
in *Period Piece*). These street
cleaners seem to be trying to
put as much as possible
down the drain.

283. Dolgelly Fire Brigade in 1909, a proud and confident body, but in the days of horse-drawn fire engines many a house was burned to the ground before the engine arrived and country houses sometimes possessed their own fire brigade.

A magnificent steam fire engine (284); the Oxford Fire Brigade on parade in 1890 (285). The modern steam fire engines, pride of the force, were at the front, the horse drawn engines at the rear, the tricyclists ready to dash ahead with hose and ladders.

▲ 286. The St Giles Fair at
Oxford when it still kept
some of its medieval
atmosphere. It is held to this
day every October.

◀ 287. Helping the police with
their inquiries c.1902.

▶ 288. The bustling forum of
Whitby market-place in
1913. None of the shoppers
seems to have noticed the
men mending the clock
tower.

▲ 290. A rare photograph taken over the walls of Portland prison, c.1894. Th[e] little groups of marching prisoners, with their dark-uniformed warders a[t] the rear, are dwarfed by th[e] huge blocks of Portland stone.

▲ 289. A typical photograph of the folk who assembled on the streets of an Edwardian country town. King Street, Maidenhead in 1903, sold Well-Made Brooms, Carbolic Soap Powder, Disinfectants, Oil Stoves in Variety by the Best Makers.

◀291. Convicts at Princeton, Dartmoor, c.1901. The prisoners on their way out of the gate shielded their faces from the photographer.

◄ Laundry girls (c.1890) at the St Marylebone Charity School for Girls, working on duckboards (292); the kitchen at the same school (293). Hot water had to be heated in the copper, while all the cooking was done on the huge solid fuel range. This was one of the many schools supported by voluntary contributions or by the parish, or both, which provided education for poor children. These schools later often became board schools.

▲ 294. 'Waiting the result' – a scene during the great dock strike of 1889, 19 August – 14 September. The dockers were claiming 6d an hour, with a minimum of four hours' work.

▲ 295. Sunday at
Scarborough, c.1897. In spite
of their finery, the ladies had
to pick their way through
horse droppings. Before
photographs were published
horse droppings were often
touched out by the
photographer in the
developing room.

▶ 296. A Salvation Army
parade, c.1896.

▲ 297. Photographers getting ready to photograph a parade in Shanklin, Isle of Wight, c. 1913.

▶ 298. An Oxford procession of dons.

▲ 299. The opening of the Blackwall Tunnel by the Prince of Wales (later Edward VII) on 22 May 1897. Work had begun in 1892 under the engineer Binnie. When completed it was the largest tunnel of its kind in the world. The *Graphic*, reporting the event, mentioned that there had been 'only' seven men killed during the work. The gateways were designed by T. Blashill, Architect to the Council. The Prince and Princess of Wales drove right through the tunnel in their carriage.